Cou

Dog Walks

Peak District - North
Dark Peak Area

www.countrysidedogwalks.co.uk

First published in December 2013 by **Wet Nose Publishing Ltd**,
Reprinted 2016
All enquiries regarding sales telephone: 01824 704398
email cdw@wetnosepublishing.co.uk
www.countrysidedogwalks.co.uk
ISBN 978-0-9573722-5-2

Contents

Introduction

The twenty walks included in this book are all designed so that you and your wet nosed friend have a really enjoyable time. Where there are stiles, they are specially designed with lift gates for dogs. At a quick glance there is information at the beginning of each walk to tell you what to expect and what you may need to take with you. The descriptive guides will also warn of any roads ahead or areas of livestock so that you can get your dog on the lead well in advance.

Dogs just love to explore new places. They really enjoy the new smells and carry themselves a little higher with the added excitement. Going to new places gets you and your dog out and about, meeting new people and their dogs. It is important to socialise dogs, as they will be more likely to act in a friendly manner towards other dogs as they gain confidence.

The stunning pictures in this book are just a taster of what you can see along the way. Many of the walks have fantastic views and scenery. Some of the walks are wooded, offering shade on those hot summer days.

The walks are graded Easy, Medium and Challenging. They are all around one to three hours long, depending on your and your dog's pace. You may start with the easy ones and work up to the challenging walks depending on your and your dog's fitness. Different dog breeds and dog age must be taken into account when you decide which walks to do.

Different breeds of dog have different levels of fitness. For example, bulldogs can only do short walks whereas a border collie or a springer spaniel are extremely energetic and difficult to tire out. It is recommended that you do some research on the breed of dog that you own to get to know what sort of exercise that they require.

You may have a walk that you are happy doing with your dog every day, but this book will show you new areas to explore with a change of scenery and a chance to meet new people and their dogs. Dogs love new places to visit and you will see the change in them as they explore the new surroundings, taking in the new smells with delight. You will fulfil both your life and your dog's just by trying somewhere new.

Some of the walks include bridleways, so you may encounter horses and cyclists. It is important to put your dog on a lead if you see horses approach. It is always helpful to say hello to the riders as they near so that the horse realises that you are not a threat.

The Peak District National Park

In 1951 the Peak District was the first area in the UK to be designated as a National Park. It lies in central and northern England, mainly in Derbyshire but covering small areas of Staffordshire, South and West Yorkshire, Cheshire and Greater Manchester.

The majority of land within the National Park is privately owned, consisting mostly of agricultural land. The National Trust own 12%, and the National Park Authority own 5%, several water companies are also major land owners, however the National Park Authority oversees land management throughout the park and planning restrictions protect the area from inappropriate development and land use.

The north (Dark Peak) and south (White Peak) differ greatly. The north is dominated by vast open moorland, with several reservoirs and forest plantations. The exposed bedrock is mostly gritstone which is dark in colour, which can be seen throughout, with many cliff faces, rock stacks and rock formations. The south has many dales and steep sided natural woodland, with rivers flowing through the bottom. The bedrock is mostly limestone, which is white in colour and is also highly visible with many cliff faces rising up from the valley floor.

Visitors to the National Park would be forgiven in thinking that they are miles from any town or city, but in fact the cities of Manchester and Sheffield lie on the boundaries, sandwiching the National Park in the middle.

Ground Nesting Birds

Watch out for vulnerable ground nesting birds during 1st of March until the end of July. Dogs that stray off the main paths may disturb birds and chicks, possibly killing them or breaking eggs. Species to look out for are Sky larks, Meadow pipits, Curlew, Red and Black grouse, Snipe and Pheasants.

Some if not all of these birds are declining in numbers, due partly to their vulnerability when nesting. Dogs are a threat to them, even if treading on them unintentionally. Some other threats are foxes, badgers, stoats, weasels, birds of prey and crows.

Please help to protect these birds during the nesting season by keeping your dog on the paths when walking in open areas such as grassland, moors, heathland and scrub.

Rivers

Some dogs love water and will think nothing of plunging into the river. With the extreme weather conditions over the last few years, a river that may be safe for your dog to swim in can change in a matter of hours to become a swollen torrent that could wash your dog away. Please be careful when near rivers if there have been heavy periods of rain or if they look swollen or fast flowing. It is best to put your dogs on the lead, until you have assessed the situation.

Livestock

If you find that you need to cross a field with cattle or horses and they seem interested in you or your dog it is recommended within the Countryside Code to let your dog off the lead. Never try to get between livestock and your dog. Your dog will get out of a situation a lot more easily with speed than you can. It is usually only cattle with young calves that are a threat, or young heifers or bullocks that tend to get a little inquisitive. They will usually stop when they get close to you or your dog.

Most horses will come over for a fuss but a small proportion do have a problem with dogs. They may see them as a threat and will act to defend the herd. Horses that are out with a rider are completely different as they are not defending the herd, and as long as you keep a safe distance there should not be a problem.

Sheep are not a danger to you, but your dog can be a danger to them. Where sheep are grazing it is vital that you have your dog on a lead or under very close control. You will know your dog, but if you are unsure it is better to play safe and keep your dog on a lead. It is important always to have your dog on a lead when around lambs. Lambs have a higher pitched bleat and can be the size of a cat, and your dog may act differently amongst them.

Ticks

If you have been walking in areas where sheep graze you should check your dog for ticks. They must be removed as soon as possible. It is best to use tick tweezers, which are specially designed to remove the head and leg parts of the tick. Ticks can carry diseases and the longer they remain latched on to your dog the more the chance of spreading infections.

Forests

The forest walks in this book are a changing landscape, which makes them unique and interesting. Descriptions may change with time, for instance a path may be described as being in the shade of the forest, but as this is a worked forest a section could be clear felled at any time. Another change over the years could be where a view is described across a previously felled area. This could then be planted up and trees grown blocking the views. Paths may change but this is less likely. On rare occasions the Forestry Commission may temporarily close paths due to forest works but again this is even less likely on a weekend. Any changes to the path networks that may occur after the date of print will be updated on our website.

Does your dog fetch a stick?

Most dogs love sticks and will pick them up without any encouragement from their owners. Vets and dog trainers recommend that you should not throw sticks for dogs. They can cause nasty injuries, sometimes fatal as the stick can pierce the throat, or rebound off the ground and cause harm to your dog.

Please clean up after your dog

Always be prepared, having dog bags with you at all times. Once you have cleaned up after your dog, please keep the bag, until you see a bin. If there are no bins provided, then take it away with you to a roadside bin. Dog bags that are discarded on the paths or in the bushes are unpleasant and unsightly and will not degrade.

1. Dovestone

Medium - 2.4 miles - 1hr 30min

This is a beautiful walk, which passes the striking Dovestone Reservoir, and then follows Chew Brook amongst wonderful rock crags and heathland. After an ascent passing a large boulder stone and facing crocodile-like rock crags above known as Whimberry Stones Brow, you will reach a long distance path 'The Oldham Way'. There are wonderful views of the surrounding countryside and over the reservoir. There may be sheep grazing throughout this walk. There is a stile, with a lift gate, where extra large breeds of dog may have difficulty passing through. Ground-nesting birds will be present during March until the end of July. Your dog will find plenty of water along the way.

How to get there – From Staleybridge, take the A635 towards Mossley. Continue, passing through Mossley, following signs for Greenfield. On passing through Greenfield, you will pick up brown signs for Dovestone Reservoir.

Grid Reference – SE 013014

Parking – Pay and display RSPB

Facilities – There are toilets in the car park

You will need – Dog leads, dog bags

The Walk

1 From the car park, go to the furthest end from the entrance and ascend the steps to reach the dam wall. There are beautiful views across the reservoir and the surrounding hills. Turn right on the tarmac path. Pass the sailing club building on your left and then you will pass the end of the reservoir. Your dog can enjoy a cool drink here on hot days.

Continue along the tarmac path, passing the sailing club parking bay. Pass through a kissing gate, keeping your dog under close control or on a lead, as there may be sheep grazing. Continue on the tarmac path, with a stone wall and farmland with mature trees on your right and a boat store on your left. Ignore a gate on your left and continue towards the hilly ridge ahead, known as Chew Hills.

2 Before going over a bridge take the footpath on the right, following beside Chew Brook on your left, where your dog can have a dip to cool off. Ascend gradually, passing scattered glacial boulders and well-spaced mature trees. Pick your way around and over the rocky boulders. You will pass a small weir in the river and then the river widens, flowing around and over boulders, creating a wonderful scene.

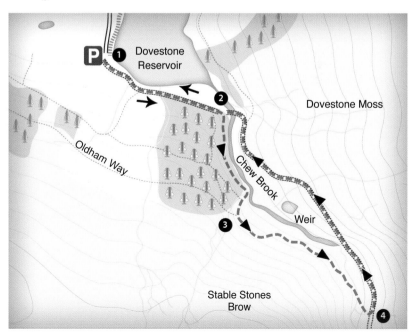

Veer to the right when near to a large square rock crag, passing next to the crag on your left. Continue on the well-worn path, passing over a stile with a lift gate for your dog. From 31st March to 31st July you should keep your dog on the path to prevent him/her causing harm to ground-nesting birds. There are also sheep grazing. Continue ascending straight ahead, heading towards the crocodile-like crags on the skyline, known as Wimberry Stones Brow.

❸ On meeting another path, turn left, joining the Oldham Way long distance path. This path is level and cuts across the hillside amongst the bracken, heather and bilberry and many glacial boulders. There are spectacular views as you look left across the valley, over the reservoir to the hills beyond.

Continue along the path for a while, where you will cross a footbridge, and follow the worn path, which meets a stock fence on your left and then ascends once again. **❹** On reaching a tarmac path, turn left and cross over a stile, letting your dog pass through the lift gate on the right hand side of the gate.

The path now descends, passing a retaining wall with large blocks of stone. You can enjoy the views as you descend, amongst the stunning scenery. As the path switches from gravel to tarmac, you can appreciate the silence it brings, when the crunch of gravel is left behind.

As you descend, the area will become dominated by bracken. The path will descend quite steeply, and on reaching level ground, cross a bridge over the brook. You will reach a familiar path; continue on this path where you will eventually return to the car park.

2. Longdendale Trail   Medium - 4.2 miles - 2hrs

This circular walk skirts around Torside Reservoir, meeting briefly with the water's edge. There are woodland sections and flower-rich grassy banks. A section of the walk covers part of the Longdendale Trail, which is a long distance footpath. This section of the walk brings beautiful views and can be popular with cyclists. You may also encounter horses as it is a bridleway. There is a firing range at the far end of the Longdendale Trail, so keep your dog on a lead if you think that the noise may cause him to bolt. There is a short section of ascent, through heather into beautiful woodland. There are many streams and pools for your dog to take a drink. There is a short section where there may be livestock and there are a couple of busy roads to cross.

How to get there – From Glossop take the B6105 Woodhead road, signed for Barnsley. Continue on this road and on reaching the reservoir on your left, look for the car park on your right hand side.

Grid Reference – SK 068983
Nearest Postcode – SK13 1JF

Parking – Torside Car Park pay and display

Facilities – There are toilets in the car park

You will need – Dog lead, dog bags

The Walk

❶ Ensure that you have your dog on a lead while in the car park, as the road is busy. From the car park, go to the furthest end from the road, heading for the left hand corner. Pass through the gate, entering into a memorial woodland. Ascend gradually. Pass through another gate, turning left to enter onto the Longdendale Trail, which is wooded on both sides with clearings which provide wild flower glades and meadows. Cyclists and horses share the path, therefore keep your dog safe, under close control or on a lead.

There are views in the clearings of the hilly countryside on your right and a little further along the path you will see the reservoir on your left. You will soon pass a beautiful clear pond on your right. Your dog will enjoy a cool drink and a dip in the water. You will pass a wildlife pond immediately after, which is vegetated with lilies and flag iris.

The path has lots of butterflies during sunny, summer afternoons and you can hear the crickets in the long grass. You will pass another crystal-clear pond on your right a little further along. You will be parallel to the road below, a little further on, and for a short section the boundary wall is low. Take care that your dog doesn't jump over and reach the road. A stock fence will soon replace the wall again.

You will hear a waterfall on your right, hidden from view by the trees. Put your dog on a lead when you reach the stone wall on the right. Take the next path on the left, which switches back and meets the road.

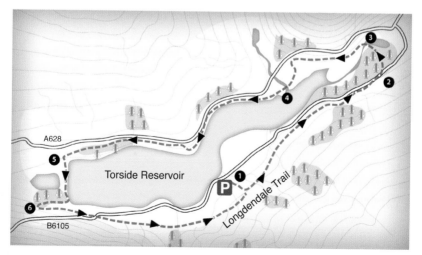

2 Pass through the kissing gate and cross the road with care.

Pass through another kissing gate opposite and descend the wide track. There is a river on your right where dogs can get water, just before you enter into the forest. Keep your dog on a lead or under close control, because this is a site entrance to the water works.

As you reach the fencing, look to your right facing the fence, where you will see water flowing from a reservoir above, flowing down like an enormous water feature. **3** Cross the bridge over the reservoir dam. Descend the steps and walk on the narrow path, which is raised, with wild flowers on each side. You will have views of the reservoir ahead and across the valley. Please prevent your dog going into the wildlife reserve on the left.

Ignore a couple of paths on your left. There is an overflow channel on your right with steep sloped sides. Take care if you have a dog that is not very athletic as he may struggle to get out, if entering into the water.

There is beautiful scenery in all directions. You will pass a lovely crafted stone arched bridge. Ignore the path that crosses the bridge and continue straight ahead. Ignore a desire line to the road and continue on the gravel path, which descends to reach a kissing gate.

Pass through the kissing gate and turn left, heading towards the water's edge, with stock fence on your left. You will now be walking along the edge of the water. **4** Cross a concrete bridge over a canalised section. Dogs that love water will take advantage of this section. This is the closest to the water you will get so you may wish to stop a while and make the most of it.

Continue along the path between the bracken. The path can get a little encroached in areas. You will reach a stone wall on your right, with some gaps which are stopped by post and rail fencing. The edge of the reservoir is laid-stone blocks which are sloped.

For a short section you will hear a busy road to your right. Keep your dog under close control to keep him safe. You will soon be under the shade of the trees. There is another water channel on your right, again with steep sides, so unless your dog is athletic, keep him on the path.

You can relax a little further along, when you meet with a stock fence on your right. The reservoir is below you now. The path meets a bridge and after crossing the bridge, pass through a kissing gate and ascend the steps into Tinsel School Wood. The path is a little steep in places. There is an abundance of bilberry and heather, with some wood sage.

On reaching the top there is a bench, where you can take a rest. Now follow the path through the mixed broadleaved woodland. The path will descend a little through the woods. The path will get quite close to a main road on the other side of the wall. Keep an eye out for your dog and ensure he doesn't jump the wall.

The path cuts across the wooded hillside, with the channel of water at the bottom of the hill. Cross a stile, with a lift gate for dogs, on reaching the stone wall. You will follow a stone wall now on your left.

Cross a footbridge over a steam where your dog can cool off. Pass through a kissing gate and turn left, then through a gate into pine trees, following the undulating path. You will now have the stone wall on your left and a stock fence on your right.

Pass through a gap in the stone wall and continue. Watch that your dog doesn't jump the wall on your left, as there is a drop on the other side. Pass through another gap in the stone wall and then pass through a gate. Descend the steps and cross a footbridge. Another set of steps brings you to the dam wall.

❺ Cross the dam wall, where you will be walking between two reservoirs. If your dog is capable of jumping the wall, keep him on a lead. At the end of the dam, turn right and go through the kissing gate, putting your dog on a lead before hand, or under very close control as there may be sheep grazing.

Go straight ahead through the woodland pasture, following the worn path. Take the next left turn, passing through a tunnel, with an ancient cobble stone path. Turn left, following the way markers for Longdendale Trail.

Put your dog on a lead on reaching the kissing gate, pass through and continue straight ahead. Turn right onto a gravel path. You will soon reach the busy main road. The path has an abundance of wild flowers in the grassy glades. Pass through a gateway and continue straight ahead for a few strides. On reaching the road, cross, taking great care, and take the path on the opposite side.

You are now back on the Longdendale Trail. Continue to follow the trail, passing grassy glades and woodlands. At a clearing in the trees, you will have fantastic views looking over the reservoir and hills beyond. On reaching back at the stone wall, turn left into the car park.

3. Langsett Bank

Easy - 2 miles - 1hr

This is a wonderful circular walk, which follows the edge of Langsett Reservoir through the woodland. At the furthest point your dog can have a dip in the river, before returning through forest with a small detour to an old quarried area, with heathland and a pond. There is plenty of water along the way, no roads and only a short section that may have livestock.

How to get there – From Sheffield, take the A61 signed for Barnsley. Turn left following signs for Manchester and A616. Turn left at the junction onto the A616, pass Underbank Reservoir on your left and continue until reaching Langsett Reservoir on your left (signed by a parking and picnic symbol a little before).

Grid Reference – SE 210004
Nearest Postcode – S36 4GY

Parking – Free in the car park

Facilities – There are toilets in the car park

You will need – Dog leads

The Walk

❶ From the car park with your back to the entrance, take a path on your right that runs parallel with the car park, heading away from the road. When you reach a stone wall ignore the left and right path, and take the middle path. Follow the stone wall on your left.

At the fork go left, descending into the forest. On reaching another path turn right. The path will descend and you will have views of Langsett Reservoir on your left. **❷**

Ignore a footpath on your right and continue on the well-made path, amongst the Scots pines and silver birch, with bracken understory. Ignore another path on your right. You will pass some oaks amongst the pine trees.

Shortly after passing the reservoir the path will begin to ascend a little and the pines will give way to oak and silver birch woodland. Ignore the ascending footpath on your right and continue straight ahead.

On meeting a cobble path turn left, descending towards a bridge. Cross the bridge and turn right. Put your dog on a lead or under close control as there may be sheep grazing and ground-nesting birds once through the gate. Pass through the gate where your dog can get access to the river.

❸ After you have enjoyed the river, turn back through the gate and over the bridge. Ascend the cobble path, ignoring the paths on the right, and continue into the woods. You will reach a concrete section of the path; take the path on

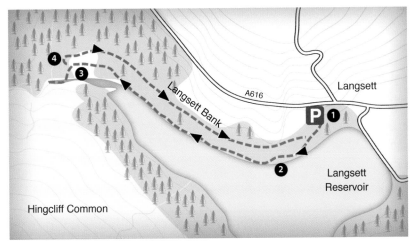

the right here, which is way marked. **4** There is a gentle ascent, with pine trees on your left and mixed broadleaved woodland on your right.

Ignore a set of steps on your left and continue on the path. There is a stone wall on your left, and pine trees now on both sides of the path. The path then descends and you will pass a path on your left in the dip of the hill. After ascending some steps you will be on the edge of the forest, with bilberry and gorse followed by bracken on your left.

Pass through an old entrance/gap in the stone wall, with trees on both sides once again, on a path which cuts across the hillside. You will pass exposed rock on your left, and a little further along the woods are dominated by silver birch. For a short detour, take the next path on your left, which brings you into a forest clearing, with heathland and an old quarry pond. You can sit for a while on the bench, while your dog enjoys the water.

Then turn back out of the clearing, turning left on the original path to continue through the woodland. Ignore another path on your left and continue, where you will be on the edge of the forest once again. The path descends a little, then just before the path begins to ascend, when you reach a stone wall on your right, put your dog on a lead as you will soon approach the car park.

4. Broomhead

Easy - 2.3 miles - 1hr

This is a fantastic circular walk, where (except for a short section) there is no livestock, so you can enjoy a relaxing walk, without the tugging of a lead. The first section is along a quiet bridleway, so you may encounter horses. You will then pass the dam with a lovely water tower, with stunning views of the valley, wonderful hilly countryside, and across to More Hall Reservoir. You then have a lovely woodland walk, following the edge of the reservoir.

How to get there – From the A628 Woodhead Pass head towards Sheffield then at the roundabout take the A616 signed Sheffield and Stocksbridge. Turn right when reaching a road signed Midhopestones and Bradfield. Continue on this road, until you see a sign for Bolsterstone. Turn left here, and on reaching the end of the road, turn left again, following for Bolsterstone. Take a road on your left, New Road, before going over a road bridge. Continue on this road, until you see the lay-by on your left.

Grid reference – SK 262956

Parking – Free in the lay-by

Facilities – There are no facilities

You will need – Dog leads, dog bags

Countryside Dog Walks - Peak District, North (Dark Peak Area)

The Walk

❶ Follow the bridleway at the end of the lay-by, with a hedgerow on your right and estate fencing on your left, with trees on both sides. As the path veers away from the road, the trees broaden on your right, becoming mixed broadleaved woodland.

Ignore the footpaths on your right and continue. On reaching a dam at the end of the reservoir, put your dogs on leads or under close control before going through the gate, because there are sheep on the next section of the walk.

❷ Follow the tarmac path beside the dam wall. There are stunning views on your right, looking across the valley to More Hall Reservoir which is surrounded by trees and beautiful countryside, and on your left across the length of Broomhead Reservoir. Ahead there is the water tower and to the right of the tower there is a drop at the end of the grass, so beware if you have excitable dogs.

On reaching close to the water tower go to the side of the estate fencing and pass through the gate on your left. **❸** Cross the bridge, ensuring that your dog doesn't jump over the wall, and turn left onto a grassy track.

You will now be near to the edge of the reservoir with woodlands on your right. The path will soon go through the woodland, and after crossing over a

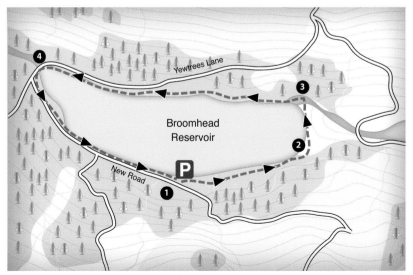

concrete bridge, continue straight ahead following close to the reservoir for some distance. The path is undulating with grassy glades and you will cross several footbridges over streams.

Just as you pass a path on the right, you will pass close to a road with only a post and rail fence, so your dog may get onto the road. Keep him under close control on this section. On meeting a fork in the path, take either path as they both meet further along. You will reach an exit onto the road a little further along, so be ready to put your dog on a lead as soon as you near the post and rail fencing. There isn't a gate, just a gap, so your dog can reach the road.

❹ On reaching the road turn left, cross the road bridge and then turn left again, heading back into the woodland. Continue straight ahead, ignoring a minor path on your left. Keep dogs under close control because you will continue close to the road to begin with.

The path will veer away from the road and follow close to the water's edge once again (depending on the water level). You will pass a clearing where you will gain views across the length of the reservoir.

Just after the clearing you will reach a fork on the path. Take the right path, keeping your dog under close control once again as you near the road. You will pass a gap in the post and rail fencing and continue straight ahead, crossing the boardwalk. Continue on the path adjacent to the road, passing over a few streams and another exit onto the road. Continue for some distance until you ascend some steps, putting your dog on a lead, and enter the parking bay.

5. Agden Reservoir

Easy - 2.7 miles - 1hr 30min

This lovely circular walk starts with a river. After crossing a footbridge, there are steep steps to climb. You walk along a quiet lane, which offers wonderful views over the reservoir. The reservoir is wooded for much of the walk and there are no livestock. Another quiet road brings you back to your car. There is water along the way for your dog.

How to get there – From Sheffield take the A57 heading towards the Snake Pass, and Glossop, turning right following signs for Strines Moor. Continue on this road, passing the Strines Inn on your left, then take the right hand turn, heading for Bradfield and Dungworth. Turn left, following the parking sign and recycle centre, just before reaching the village.

Grid Reference – SK 260919

Parking – Free in the car park

Facilities – There are facilities in the village, just beyond the car park.

You will need – Dog leads, dog bags

The Walk

❶ From the car park go back to the entrance and turn right. Take the stone slab footpath with the car park on your right and a field on your left walking between the stone walls. On meeting the river, ignore the footbridge and continue alongside the river on your right, under the shade of mixed broadleaved trees.

Cross the footbridge and ascend a flight of steps, with mature oak, beech, horse chestnut and sycamore. Pass a gap in the stone wall and turn left. Put your dog on a lead and continue on the path with a garden fence on your left and a stone wall on your right. **❷** On reaching the quiet road turn left. The road is tree lined, with a stone wall on your right with woodland over the other side.

You will soon see exceptional views of the reservoir on your left. Continue along the road, where you will pass an old stone water trough, still in working order, with liverworts growing over it. Cross a road bridge then a little further along you will see a break in the stone wall on your left. **❸** Turn left here and pass through the entrance into Agden Reservoir.

Cross a short sleeper bridge over a gully and follow the path straight ahead, passing the Scots pine trees, beside the reservoir on your left. You will then

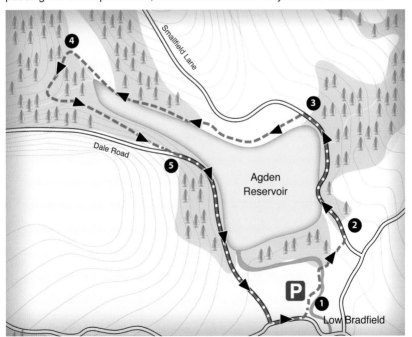

pass oaks and rowan trees with bracken understory. Take a path on your right, ascending for a short distance and pass through the kissing gate.

Turn left on a level path with iron rail fencing on your left. Ignore the narrow path on your right and continue. There is a drop on the other side in places. Be sure to keep your dog under close control here so he doesn't jump over the wall.

You will pass between two sets of old stone gate posts. There is a river down below on your left, with yellow flag iris in the spring and early summer. The woods are dominated by oak and silver birch, with bilberry understory.

4 Just before you reach stock fencing on your left with a sign for Agden Bog Nature Reserve, take a narrow path on your left, which descends down the bank towards the river. Go through a gate and cross a footbridge, and follow the well-worn path, beside the stone wall on your right.

You will pass a boggy area on your left, where you may see flag iris growing. On reaching a stone wall, pass through a gate and turn left. Ascend into the mixed broadleaved and coniferous woodland. The path then levels out and cuts across the hillside with the river below on your left, following a dilapidated wall on your right to begin with.

The path will ascend once again, but gently. A little further along, as the path levels out once more, take the descending path on your left. You will now be beside the reservoir below. You will pass beside a stone wall on your left, and there are mature oaks with bilberry, bracken and ferns in the understory. Continue to follow the undulating, well-worn path, with the wooded hillside on your right.

The bank on your left is steep in places down to the water's edge. You will pass beside a neat stone wall on your right. The path will become narrow as you pass between holly. Bracken and ferns then dominate the area. You will soon reach close to the water's edge once again, where your dogs can get a drink.

Keep dogs under close control now as there is an exit onto the road just a little further along, just before you reach near to the dam. Take this exit, turning left on to the road. You will pass a beautifully designed house on the left.

Descend on the road, passing between farmland and on reaching a junction turn left. Then a little further along take the next road on the left, which will bring you to the car park.

6. Dale Dike Reservoir

Easy - 3.3 miles - 1hr

This is a great circular walk, which skirts around Dale Dike reservoir. The walk is almost entirely within beautiful mixed woodland, with agricultural land adjacent in parts, where there are views across the hilly countryside. In the distance bird scarers can go off at times, which may startle your dog, so you may need to keep him on a lead until you are confident that he won't bolt if they are in action. There is water all the way for your dog to get a drink.

How to get there – From Sheffield, follow for Manchester on the A57 and take the Strines Moor turn off on your right. Pass the Stines Inn on your left and continue. Take the next right hand turn signed for Bradfield and Dungworth. You will find the lay-by just after passing houses on your right hand side of the road.

Grid Reference – SK 245920

Parking – Free in the lay-by

Facilities – There are no facilities

You will need – Dog leads

The Walk

❶ From the lay-by climb over a step in the stone wall and descend the wide track with mixed trees on both sides. There are lots of foxgloves in the summer months. Just as the path levels out you will pass an interpretation panel, which tells the story of the Dale Dike disaster.

You will see the great dam ahead, and to your left a newly planted woodland. There are trees and meadows on your right. You will pass a detached house on your far right. Ignore a path on the left, which descends and continue straight ahead, on the level path.

After passing a stone wall on your right the area opens out, with newly planted trees. Ignore a gate straight ahead and take a path to the right of it. Ensure your dog is on a lead and pass through a small kissing gate. There may be sheep grazing here. Continue straight ahead towards the stone wall opposite and turn right on reaching it. At the end of the stone wall you will see another small kissing gate.

❷ Pass through the kissing gate (there is a dog lift gate on the far side of the gate if your dog is large) and continue on the path, with a stock fence on your right and the reservoir on your left. There is no stock grazing on this section of the walk. The path is tree lined on your left. Dogs can get access to the water easily a little further along.

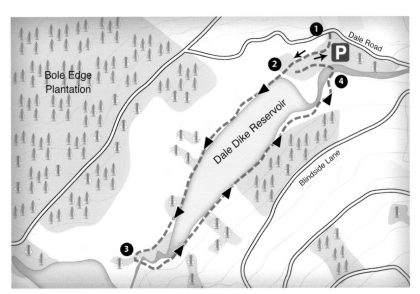

The path follows beside the reservoir with a stone wall on your right. Trees line the path on both sides. Small dogs may pass through the gap in the fencing ahead, so if they are likely to stray after sheep in the fields, keep them on a lead for the next section of the walk. At the end of the stone wall you will see a beach area on your left. Once your dogs have enjoyed the water, continue along the path with estate fencing on your right.

There are mixed broadleaved trees, which offer shade on hot days. The area will widen out once again, with mature trees and bracken. When the water in the reservoir is low, the trees on the left look like mangroves, with the roots raised above the ground. Keep to the path, stopping at intervals to enjoy the water. There are several streams flowing under the path as you continue, offering dogs an ample supply of fresh water. There is a mix of stone wall and estate fencing on your far right, so keep little, mischievous dogs under close control.

There are many geese and ducks enjoying the reservoir. On nearing a stone wall on your right, take either path ahead passing between bracken, as they re-join further ahead. At the end of the reservoir the path will veer to the right. The woodland is mostly Scots pine. There is a river below on your left, which meanders, and there is an ox-bow in the river a little further along. The trees are well spaced with grasses and bramble growing on the ground.

❸ On meeting the river, cross a footbridge and turn left, keeping dogs under close control as there may be sheep grazing here. Keep going straight ahead, as you join another path. Continue on the worn path beside the river, ignoring paths on your right.

The path cuts across a hillside, which is abundant with bilberry. The river looks still now as it meets with the reservoir. A stream crosses under the path and then over rocks, tumbling into the reservoir.

Ignore a path on the right and continue, where you will see a beach area, giving access to the water. Continue along the path, with farmland and mature parkland trees on the other side of the stone wall to your right. You will reach the water's edge in places along the path on your left, and after passing the farmland there is another wood.

A clearing in the trees provides views over the reservoir to the hilly countryside beyond. Ignore a path on your right and continue through trees and glades, where on sunny, summer days, butterflies flutter in search of nectar.

The wall on your right turns a corner, but the woodland continues with no boundary wall. As you reach close to the dam, you pass a lovely stone building on your left. You then pass a bridge with fine metalwork on your left on reaching the dam. Continue on the path through the trees, looking carefully as the path is no longer clear. Continue in the same direction and you will reach a set of steps on your left. **❹** Keep your dog under close control now as below the second set of steps there is a pumping station, which sucks water causing dangerous currents. Descend the stone steps, amongst rhododendrons and pine trees. Continue along the path where you will reach a second set of steps.

At the bottom of the steps turn right and continue on the path, ensuring that your dog does not enter the water here. Cross a bridge at a weir and then ascend the path, where you leave the woodlands behind. Continue through a new tree plantation, heading towards the dam. The path bends before reaching the dam. You will meet a familiar path. Turn right and ascend the path back to the road.

7. Upper Derwent

Challenging - 4.6 miles - 2hrs

A walk following the main paths through wonderful forest and woodland, passing a well designed water tower. Some of the paths are also popular with cyclists. As you leave the main path, a steep ascent through moorland brings you out into the open with wonderful views over the reservoirs. Here you will be away from the hustle and bustle and will hear nothing but bees buzzing busily amongst the heathland. There may be sheep grazing so you will need to keep your dog on a lead. There are no roads, other than access tracks.

How to get there – From Glossop take the Snake Pass A57, following signs for Sheffield. Continue for some distance and turn left following the brown sign for Derwent Valley just before going over a road bridge, which crosses the Ladybower Reservoir. Continue past a car park on your left and several parking bays on your right, until reaching the main car park.

Grid Reference – SK 172893

Parking - Pay and display in the main car park

Facilities – There are toilets, a gift shop, café and visitor centre in the car park

You will need – Dog lead, dog bags

The Walk

❶ From the visitor centre, face the entrance door, and take the path on your right that passes between the post and rail fence. Turn left, walking between the fencing, passing the picnic benches on your left. The path descends, with a river below on your right. Ignore a path on your left. On reaching an access road, turn right.

Pass over a road bridge, crossing a river, and continue along the road. There is an impressive dam on your left with beautiful architecture, and mixed broadleaved woodland on your right. **❷** Just after the bend in the road, take a footpath on your left. Don't go through the kissing gate, but follow the way marker signed Derwent Dam East Tower.

The path ascends gradually through mixed broadleaved woodland, with switchbacks to lessen the gradient. On meeting a path turn left. Now the path is on level ground, passing between the rhododendrons. You will pass the dam on your left. Continue between the rhododendrons, ascending a little once again.

Pass through a kissing gate, and continue straight ahead, where you will see the reservoir on your left. Oak trees now dominate the woodland on your right. Ignore a path on your right, keep your dog under close control and then cross another road bridge. There are drops over the other side of the walls.

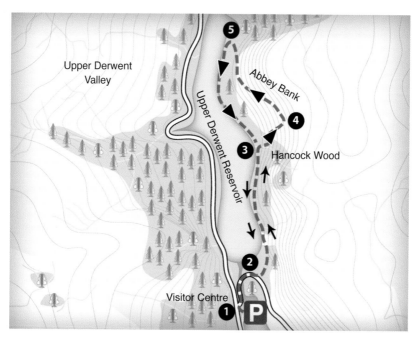

The path is popular with cyclists, so it is best to keep your dog under close control. There are views where the trees allow, across the reservoir and the surrounding hills. Continue on this path for some distance.

❸ Look out for a footpath on the right (after about 20 minutes), signed to Bradfield and Strines, ascending into the woods, with a stream below on your right. Pass through a gate into Walkers Clough – High Peak Estate. Dogs must be kept under close control or on a lead as there may be sheep. Please keep your dog on the path during nesting season 1st March – July 31st. Continue beside a stone wall on your right, and then the path veers to the left. The path ascends quite steeply, with rough, loose stone, between the bracken. The path zig-zags to lessen the gradient. You will pass the end of a dilapidated stone wall on your right, where you leave the dense bracken, entering into a vast open area with grasses and bilberry.

The path turns a sharp left, levelling out for a short distance. As the path ascends again, you will pass over a ruined stone wall near ground level. There are wonderful views on your left, looking across the valley and the reservoir. On reaching a cairn turn left, following the top path signed for Howden Reservoir, not the descending path. ❹

Follow the worn path amongst heather, bilberry and rushes. The path begins to descend and you will reach a dilapidated stone wall on your left. Follow the stone wall until you reach the copse of Scots pine trees on your left. Turn right, where you will see a beautiful scene, looking along the path into the valley, with bilberry and heather adding texture and colour in the foreground and then over the reservoir to the hills and woodlands beyond. The path is raised, with bilberry and heather sloping away on both sides. When you reach a stone wall, pass through a gate into mixed woodland. Follow the worn path. On reaching another path turn left, and then on meeting another wider path turn left again. ❺

Continue on this level path, with mixed woodland dominated by oak and beech. Again, this path is popular with cyclists, so keep your dog under close control. The reservoir is below on your right. Stay on this path, and further along you will pass a path on your left, where earlier you turned off. You are now on a familiar path. Pass back through the kissing gate, descending between the rhododendrons. You will reach the dam wall; take the steps on your right immediately afterwards to descend with the dam on your right. Follow the well-worn grassy path, crossing the meadow. On reaching the road turn right, then take the tarmac path on the left, which descends back to the visitor centre.

8. Tip Memorial

Easy - 1.5 miles - 45mins

This is a wonderful circular walk, passing through lovely woodlands and forest, until it reaches the edge of the Upper Derwent Reservoir. After a stop beside the water you will continue, where you will reach a memorial stone in memory of Tip, a faithful Border collie who stayed beside her dead master for 15 weeks during a harsh cold winter. Then you will continue to pass the popular visitor centre and café.

How to get there – From Glossop take the Snake Pass A57, following signs for Sheffield. Continue for some distance and turn left following the brown sign for Derwent Valley, just before going over a road bridge which crosses the Ladybower Reservoir. Follow the road until you reach the last car park on the right hand side of the road, just before reaching the main car park and visitor centre.

Grid Reference – SK 172893

Parking – Free in Derwent Overlook Car Park at the side of the road.

Facilities – There are toilets, a café and a gift shop with a visitor centre

You will need – Dog leads, dog bags

The Walk

1 Go to the road and turn right, where at the end of the parking bay you will reach a pavement. Follow the road, ignoring a path on the right and a footpath on the left. Just before reaching the No Entry sign ahead, stop and look left for a footpath. Cross the road that you have been following and take the gate into the mixed deciduous woodland.

Pass an old retaining wall on your right. There is a stream below on your left. Ignore a path on your right and continue straight ahead, ascending on the gravel path. Pass over a bridge, crossing a canalised section of the river. **2** Now turn right, ascending a couple of steps, and then follow the path which ascends gradually, following an old dilapidated wall on your far left.

The path levels off for a short section and then descends as you enter a cedar forest. The path will lead onto a wider track, where you continue straight ahead. Just as you enter into larch trees you will pass an impressive dam, with two water towers. Continue on the path, which descends gently again. Pass through a gate, putting your dog on a lead as you will approach a road. **3**

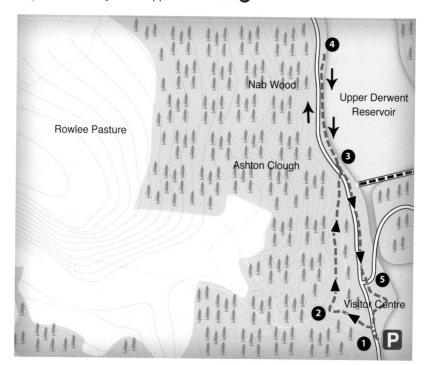

On meeting the road, cross it and turn left. Take a path on the right and follow between the reservoir and the quiet road. There may be sheep grazing in this area. You can enjoy the water's edge here for a while. ❹

Turn around, put your dog on a lead and head back to the road. Turn left at the road and continue, where you will pass through a kissing gate to avoid the cattle grid and continue along the path beside the road. You will pass the memorial for Tip the sheepdog.

Continue on the path, passing the dam, and take the footpath on the left in the middle of a parking bay. Descend the stone steps into larch woods on a worn path. Do not go down the next set of steps, but call your dog close and continue on the path, which descends to the road.

On reaching the road ensure your dog is on a lead, turn left and then take the footpath on the right. Keep your dog on a lead as you are heading to a visitor centre and there are usually a lot of ducks in the vicinity. At the fork turn left, passing the visitor centre on your right. ❺

Pass the car park, staying on the tarmac path which follows the river below on your left. As you turn round a bend, you will see Lady Bower Reservoir on your left. On reaching another path turn left, passing mature beech trees. Descend the steps and follow the worn path, crossing a footbridge. On reaching an opening, stop for a while and enjoy the view across the reservoir.

Take a path on your right, which meanders up a hill to reach a road. Ensure your dog is under close control and on a lead before reaching the road. Turn left on reaching the road and continue on a familiar path until you reach the parking bay.

IN
COMMEMORATION OF
THE DEVOTION OF
TIP.
THE SHEEPDOG WHICH STAYED
BY THE BODY OF HER DEAD
MASTER, MR. JOSEPH TAGG,
ON THE HOWDEN MOORS FOR
FIFTEEN WEEKS FROM 12TH
DECEMBER 1953 TO 27TH
MARCH 1954.

ERECTED BY PUBLIC
SUBSCRIPTION

9. Kinder Low
Challenging - 7.2 miles - 3hrs 45mins

This is a wonderful circular walk, passing beside woodland and through farmland, where after a steady climb you will cross over moorland reaching wonderful panoramic views. There is a little section of easy scrambling, where you step over boulders, then a level walk across the top of the moor, where you will pass terrific boulders and rock faces. Open peat spreads across an extensive flat area, looking purple in the distance, with lots of cotton grass and heather. It is best seen in August and September when the heather is in flower and there are no ground-nesting birds. There may be sheep grazing throughout the walk. Dogs will find water at a couple of streams, but it's best to bring water on hot days.

How to get there – From Chapel en le Frith take the A624 towards Glossop. Turn right following the road sign into Hayfield Village. Turn right onto Bank Street, following the sign for camping. Turn right again onto Kinder Road. Continue on this road, where you will see the car park on the left hand side.

Grid Reference – SK 048869 **Nearest Postcode** – SK22 2LH

Parking – Pay and display at Bowden Bridge

Facilities – There are no facilities

You will need – Dog lead, dog bags, water for your dog

Countryside Dog Walks - Peak District, North (Dark Peak Area)

The Walk

❶ Put your dog on a lead to begin this walk. From the car park, cross the road at the entrance, and go over the road bridge and turn immediate right into Hayfield Camp Site. Pass through a gate and continue along the access road, with the river on your right.

Pass a building on your left and then turn left, on the footpath signed for Highgate Head. Pass between the hedges and go through the gates, crossing the camp site. Ascend the steps and then ascend the path, passing through a gate through the stone wall, and turn left. This is a bridleway so you may encounter horses and bikes.

You will have woodland on your right and a horse paddock on your left. The path will ascend quite steeply in places, with a stone wall on both sides. You will pass Stones House Farm. There are mixed conifer and broadleaved trees on your right and views on your left and ahead of the beautiful hilly countryside.

The path will level out as you reach a right hand bend. There is a barbed wire fence now on your left and a stone wall on your right. You will reach the end of the woods. **❷** Here you will need to keep your dog on a lead or under close control, as there is livestock ahead. Pass through a gate into open farmland. Pass a stone bench on the right and continue along the path, which cuts across the hillside. There is lovely scenery in all directions here with a copse of trees to your right and mature trees scattered throughout.

The path descends to reach a quiet road. Turn right, ignore a path ahead and to your right, and continue with the descending, quiet road. There is a stock fence and woodland to your left. Ignore a path on the right and continue straight ahead.

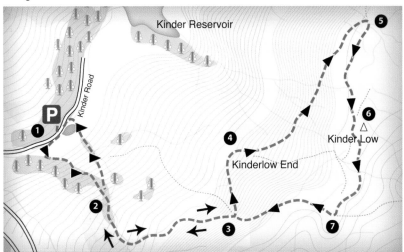

You will see a river below on your right. A little further ahead, dogs can get a drink as the path comes level with the river. Pass through a gate and continue straight ahead. Follow the road with a stone wall on your left and a stock fence and the river on your right.

Mature trees line a stretch of the road, giving welcome shade in hot weather. The road ascends here as it veers sharply to the left. A stream is accessible for your dog on the right. In summer there are floristic grass banks at the side of the road. You pass a fine stone barn and house built in 1804 on your left.

At a sharp bend in the road, continue straight ahead, passing through a gate on an ascending, stony path between stock fencing. You will pass footpaths to your left and right, continuing straight ahead ascending between the farmland.

Pass through another gate, entering the Kinder Estate. Continue straight ahead, keeping dogs under close control or on a lead as there may be sheep and during the nesting period, ground-nesting birds. Just a little further along; go through the gate on your left, signed Bridleway to Glossop. ❸

Follow the worn path through open countryside, now on a gentle ascent which becomes undulating. The path, which can get boggy in places, follows close to a well-maintained stone wall on your far left.

Pass through a gate and look carefully. You will see three paths: ignore the path turning right, and ignore a path that veers to the left and ahead towards the stone wall, but take the path in the middle, going straight ahead. ❹ The path will soon become more defined.

There are pockets of heather and cotton grass amongst the grassland. The path will soon ascend and then level out again as it cuts across the hillside, occasionally passing glacial boulders.

Another short ascent brings you past some glacial boulders, now on an undulating path. You can see a reservoir in the distance to your left and stunning stone-covered hills. Continue on this path for quite some time. You will reach an area where there are lots of glacial boulders, with different

shapes and sizes, some up-ended, scattered across the landscape. The path reaches an edge of the slope with a deep cut in the valley. This route can be tricky with dogs on a lead. When you reach close to the cutting, you will see an obvious path crossing over the rock to reach the other side.

Continue straight ahead along the worn path, with a bit of an easy scramble, choosing a route that you are comfortable with. On reaching a wide track, turn right. **❺** You will reach a larger area of exposed rock. Cross the rock, veering to the right. Continue following this wider path for some distance, passing a series of cairns (piles of rocks) amongst the rock formations and bilberry. The path is undulating with some steps.

After quite a distance you will pass areas of open peat, which spread out across the flat landscape on the left, with cotton grass in early to mid summer. **❻** You will reach a trig point, where the path is not obvious because of the exposed rock at ground level. You will be surrounded by open peat and cotton grass, from a distance it looks like a mass of purple and white. There are cairns scattered around and some large glacial boulders. Continue in the same direction that you have been going and veer slightly to the right.

You will soon see a path to the left of a large exposed rock outcrop. Follow this path, which is made of stone slabs. There is a lovely valley to your left, and a little further along you will pass beside a steep sided hill on your right as you descend. Further along again, take the path on your right, heading toward a stone wall.

❼ Go through a gate on your right and follow a stone wall on your right. There is vast grassland on your left. The path will ascend steeply for a short time. As the ground levels out you will pass through a gateway in the stone

wall. Continue ahead, now descending on a rough track. You will pass a couple of welcome streams, where dogs can get a drink. Ignore a footpath on the right and continue straight ahead.

Pass through another gate and continue with the stone wall on your right. Pass old gritstone gate posts on your left. Ignore another path on the right, and continue now on a familiar path. After passing through the gate, you will have stock fences on both sides, where you can let your dog off the lead. This path is a bridleway so you may encounter horses and bikes. There may also be farm vehicles using the path. Make sure you put your dog on the lead before reaching the road.

On reaching the road at the bend, continue straight ahead, following a familiar path for a while. You will pass the stream on your left once more, where dogs can get a drink. Continue along the road where you will reach two gates; take the gate on the right this time, leaving the familiar path now.

Follow this access road, with a river on your left. Keep to the left, ignoring a track on the right. There are trees on both sides of the road and the river crosses beneath to then be on your right.

There is a retaining wall on your left for a while and the road will begin to ascend. After passing the tree line on your left, you will see a grassy hillside. You will have views on your right of the hilly countryside, after passing the trees. Go through a gate on your left to avoid the cattle grid. There are mature ash, sycamore and beech trees on both sides of the road.

Cross over a bridge and turn left. Continue along the road, which follows the river and a stone wall on your left. The river then passes under the road and is now on your right. You will soon reach a familiar bridge. Cross this and then cross the road back to the car park.

10. Mam Tor

Challenging - 3 miles - 2hrs

This is a wonderful walk, steeped in history, as you travel over the Bronze Age hill fort and cross the spine of this wonderful 'Shivering Mountain', with awe-inspiring views across the Hope and Edale valleys. With very little effort you feel as though you are on top of the world. A clear day is a must to really appreciate this walk. There are no roads on this walk. It is likely that there will be sheep grazing throughout and possibly cattle, but as the paths are very popular the cattle should be used to people and dogs and therefore will show little interest in you.

How to get there –The car park is situated on the A6187 from Chapel en le Frith, following signs for the Blue John Cavern but turning left just before the entrance. You will then see the car park.

Grid Reference – SK 123832

Parking – Pay and Display in the National Trust Mam Nick Car Park

Facilities – There are no facilities

You will need – Dog leads, dog bags

Countryside Dog Walks - Peak District, North (Dark Peak Area)

The Walk

❶ From the car park, keeping to the left hand side and ascending away from the road, you will see a set of steps. Ensure that you have your dog on a lead, as you will be walking parallel with a road. Ascend the steps and continue on the path, parallel with the road on your left.

When you reach the road, go through a kissing gate straight ahead of you and ascend the steps where you will soon have views to your right looking across Hope Valley. As you rise a little higher you will have views across the Edale Valley on your left.

Continue to climb a little higher on the stone slabs and steps of this gentle slope. Once reaching Mam Tor you will see a trig point. You are now at the summit of this ancient hill fort. **❷**

Continue on this path to enjoy the panoramic views as you ascend and descend gently along the spine of the 'Shivering Mountain', as it is known locally because of the constant land slides.

Staying with this path until you reach the Tom Hyett memorial stone. Here take the path to your left and back (not directly left). **❸** This path will descend with views across the Edale Valley and a dilapidated stone wall on your right. A little further on ignore a path on your right and continue straight ahead, now leaving the stone wall.

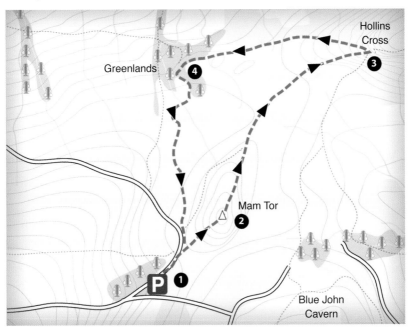

This route is quieter than the more popular route on the spine of the hill. There may be cattle grazing here. You will pass a small stream where your dog can get a drink. Pass through a gate and continue straight ahead.

The scenes are stunning here as you are surrounded by peaks. Head for a gate to pass through the stone wall, then a second gate. ❹ You are now on a gravel path passing through the High Peak Wildlife Havens. It is best to keep your dog on a lead as there may be ground-nesting birds between April and July.

Stay on the gravel path between the gorse and scrub. Your dog may seek another drink as a stream flows under the path. You won't tire of the stunning views across the valley with patchwork fields and hills.

Pass through another gateway where you leave the wildlife reserve. Continue on the path with fields and a fence line to your left and scrub to your right. Pass through a gate to continue straight ahead and then through another gate, passing a hedgerow and house to your right.

Stay on this ascending path, with a sharp bend to the left and then a bend on the right at a stone electric hut. You will have stunning views to your right. After passing through a gate follow the stone wall on your right. A stock fence will replace the stone wall.

The path veers away from the fence line as you pass an ash tree, where you then follow the well-worn trail which ascends the hill. The path will meet up again with a stone wall to your right. Remember to stop, look back at the views and take a rest.

Pass through a gate and continue ascending on a well made path. On reaching another gate, don't go through it, but continue straight ahead, where you will have climbed to your highest point. Follow on the narrow path with the fence line and road on your right. Soon you will see the stone laid path. Go right onto this path, which leads to a familiar gate. Once through the gate stay on the path that runs parallel with the road and back to the car park.

Countryside Dog Walks - Peak District, North (Dark Peak Area)

11. Lyme Park

Medium - 3 miles - 1hr 45min

This is a wonderful walk in the grounds of the beautiful, Georgian estate, now owned by the National Trust. You will pass through a deer enclosure, and then into wonderful woodland. After crossing pasture land, into wood pasture, you will have the most amazing views after a short, gradual ascent, looking over the beautiful, rolling countryside for miles. There may be sheep and deer in places. There is a quiet access road and a couple of streams for your dog.

How to get there – From Buxton, take the A6, signed for Stockport and Manchester. Lyme Park will be signed off the main road, just after leaving Disley.

Grid Reference – SJ 965825
Postcode – SK12 2NR

Parking – The parking is free, but there is an admission charge; see National Trust website for details

Facilities – There are toilets and a café, close to the car park

You will need – Dog leads, dog bags

Countryside Dog Walks - Peak District, North (Dark Peak Area)

The Walk

❶ Starting in the main car park, standing facing the kiosk/ visitor centre, turn right and go to the end of the car park, staying on the left hand side. On reaching the corner ascend the steps and go through the gate keeping your dog on a lead whilst in the Deer Reserve.

Ascend the well-made path and as you have full views of the house on your left, take the path on your right. Follow on the path, between the lime avenue. If you are lucky, you may see the fallow deer as you pass through.

❷ Once you pass through the gate on the other side you can let your dog off the lead. Continue straight ahead on the path, ascending through the mixed woodland, which is mostly beech and pine. On reaching another path turn left. Continue along the path until you reach a gate. Don't pass through the gate, but turn right.

Follow the path along the edge of the woodland, ignoring any paths on your right. Stay close to the stone wall on your left with beautiful views across the rolling countryside.

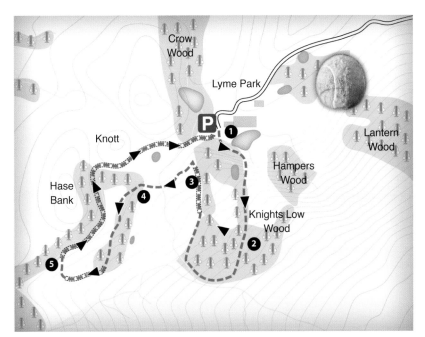

When you reach a ladder stile on your left don't go over it. Your dog can go through the gap in the stone wall to the stream on the other side to get a drink. Turn right now, staying on the edge of the woodland. On reaching a gate on your left, put your dog on a lead or under close control and pass through it. There may be sheep for the next section of the walk.

Continue straight ahead on the well-worn path, with Scots pine on your right and pasture on your left. There are views ahead of you. The path descends and as you reach a gate on your right, turn left to cross the field. ❸ The path will become more defined a little further along.

You will go over the brow of a small hill. Continue on the path, turning right when you see a gate and ladder stile going over a stone wall on your far right. Head towards the stone wall and a ladder stile. Cross over a small stream and continue until you reach the ladder stile. ❹ There is a dog flap in the gate. Cross the ladder stile and turn left. Pass through another gate into wood pasture.

You are now in a livestock free area. Take a path on your right, which veers away from the stone wall. Continue on this path, ignoring a path on your left and right. You will reach stunning views as you continue a little further. A little further along you will see a house ahead of you; this is Paddock Cottage. Continue towards the cottage. When you reach it the panoramic views are breath-taking.

Pass the cottage on your left and continue on the wide, grassy path with stunning scenery, surrounded by rolling hills and countryside. You will follow near to a stock fence on your left for some time, until you reach close to two mature oak trees. Turn right here and continue to follow the wide, grassy path.

Ignore a narrow path on your left and continue, where you will head back towards the cottage at the top of the hill. After a short distance, you will reach a wide grassy path on your left. Take this path, where you will then meet a wide track. Veer left onto this track and descend towards the woods.

❺ On reaching the woods and another path, turn right. There is a stream here, where your dog can get a drink. There are pines on your left and rhododendrons on your right, followed by an open grassy bank, with mature trees. On reaching near to a gate ahead, call your dog up close or put him on a lead. Pass through the gate and cross the car park, following the access track through the hilly pasture, where sheep may be grazing.

Go through another gate, to avoid the cattle grid, where you will reach the main car park.

12. Castleton

Challenging - 4.5 miles - 2.5hrs

This circular walk has lots to keep you interested. There are many rock crags and wonderful, dramatic rock formations, some are grassed over, blending into the hillside. You will pass through farmland, sometimes between fences, so your dog can be off the lead. There are stunning views of the surrounding landscape. There are sheep grazing throughout most of the walk and possibly cattle and horses. There are some quiet roads.

How to get there – The car park is found on the main road in Castleton on the A6187. It is the main car park and is located beside the Tourist Information and visitor centre.

Grid Reference – SK 149830
Postcode – S33 8WN

Parking – Pay and display in Cross Street car park

Facilities – There are toilets in the car park and shops/cafes in the village.

You will need – Dog lead, dog bags

The Walk

1 From the car park head back onto the road and turn left. Cross to the opposite side and continue to the sharp bend in the road and turn right into Back Street. Pass a church on your right and continue straight ahead into Market Place.

Turn left at the top of the square, and then turn right, following the sign for Cave Dale, just as you enter Pindale Road. There may be sheep for the next section of the walk, so keep dogs on leads or under close control. Pass between rocks and go through a gate onto the Limestone Way. Ascend on the rocky, stony path through the dramatic landscape, where sculptured rock faces surround you and with trees growing from the rock faces on the right.

You will reach another pinch area in the rock, and a little further along you will see a small, blocked off cave to your right. You will then pass another wider gap in the rock, where dogs will find water as it trickles across the path.

You will pass through a gate on reaching a stone wall. Look behind you at this point for fantastic views. Continue beside a stone wall on your right, ascending between hills. The path will level out for a short spell, where you pass beside old stone gate posts. You will reach another gentle ascent, where you will leave the stone wall and then pass beside another rocky outcrop.

Soon you will meet another stone wall on your right. Continue beside the stone wall for a while until the hill on your left veers away and the landscape opens out a little. Pass through a gate on your right, through the wall and continue straight ahead, through the middle of a field. On reaching another

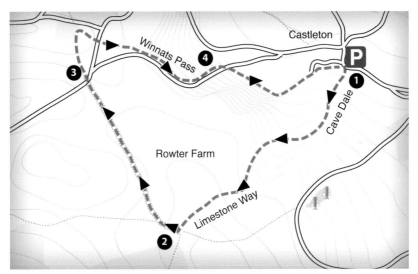

gate, again pass through the field, leaving the stone wall on the right as the path veers to the left, just after passing a finger post on your right. You should still be within sight of the stone wall, about 50m to your right. Soon you will see a farm gate ahead. Head towards the farm gate, passing a boggy pond on your right. Pass through a gap beside the gate, then between the stone wall and through a farm gate. Turn right to pass through another farm gate, following the track between the stone walls, with farmland on either side. There aren't any sheep grazing on this path, but there may be farm vehicles and horses.

2 Turn right at the corner of the stone wall to continue with the stone wall on your right and a stock fence on your left. Continue on this track for some distance, ignoring a footpath on your left and right. There may be sheep/cattle for the next section of the walk. Put your dog back on a lead or under close control and pass through a gate into another field, keeping to the tarmac path with the stone wall on your right. Pass the access path to the farm house and continue straight ahead, passing Rowter Farm camp site on your far right.

3 You will reach a farm gate ahead and a road. Pass through the gate, cross the road and take the footpath slightly to your right. There are livestock in the field here. Follow the track with a stone wall on your left; you will see Mam Tor ahead of you. Continue with the track, after passing the stone wall, passing an old quarried area on your right. You will pass a grassy path on your right. Take another grassy path on your right, just before reaching the gate in the stone wall ahead. Follow this path, which crosses the middle of the field, heading for a gate in the stone wall.

Ensure your dog is on a lead, pass through the gate, cross the road with care, and pass through a gate on the opposite side. Continue straight ahead through the field, keeping dogs on a lead or under close control, as there may be livestock and horses grazing. You will pass through a small gate. Continue with a stone wall on your right, to the edge of farmland. Pass a farm gate and farmhouse on your right and continue following the stone wall, with a road over the other side on your right.

Ignore a gate and footpath on your right that goes onto the road, and continue descending beside the stone wall. Pass through a gap beside the rocky outcrop and the stone wall and descend to the gate. Put your dogs on a lead, pass through the gate and continue through the valley, on the Winnats Pass, between the road and a stone wall. There are stunning rock formations jutting out throughout this valley, and beautiful countryside views straight ahead. You will soon be descending alongside the road, where dogs will find water from a stream as it trickles across the path. Continue amongst the stunning landscape, passing through the Speedwell Cavern car park. At the end of the car park you will reach a pavement, after a few paces, look to your right, you will see a gate on the opposite side of the road. **4** Cross the road with care and pass through the gate.

Keeping dogs on a lead or under close control, as there is livestock in this field, follow beside the stone wall on your left. There are beautiful views across the countryside, with hills and rows of neat stone walls on your left. The path will veer away from the stone wall for a short while.

You will soon be beside another stone wall on your left. A little further along, pass through a kissing gate and continue straight ahead to the edge of the field. Continue alongside the stone wall as the path descends gradually to reach a rocky path with woodland on your right. Pass through a gate and continue to descend passing between stone walls. You will reach a quiet road, passing beautiful cottages on both sides. Cross a road bridge over a river and take the next road on your left, following beside the river. At the end of the road you will reach a busy road, where you will see the car park on the opposite side.

13. Ladybower

Medium - 6 miles - 2.5hr

This is a lovely walk which passes over the dam and has a great view of the plug holes from where the water is drained. You will follow the reservoir for some time alongside the forest. There is a steep ascent for a small stretch of this walk, which then takes you across a cutting in the hillside through the forest. There are plenty of opportunities for your dog to get a drink, as there are many streams that flow under the path to the reservoir. There may be sheep grazing and you will cross a busy road near the beginning and end of the walk.

How to get there – From Hope valley follow the road towards Sheffield. Just as you enter into Bamford take the A6013 on your left, signed for Bamford. Continue through the village and a little further along the road, just before reaching the traffic lights, the car park will be on your right. From the A57 Snake Pass, on reaching the traffic lights turn onto the A6013 and the car park will be on the left.

Grid Reference – SK 202859
Nearest Post Code – S33 0AZ

Parking – Pay and Display Heatherdene Car Park

Facilities – There are toilets in the car park

You will need – Dog leads, dog bags

The Walk

1 Keep your dogs on leads to begin this walk. From the car park go to the right hand side, following the signs for pay and display. Pass the pay and display on your left, where you will see a surfaced track, take this track, passing the toilet block on your left. Pass through the gate and continue on this path, passing steps on your right. Continue between the trees and rhododendrons. When you see the dam wall on the right, take the next path on the right. Descend the steps to the main road.

Cross the road and follow the path across the dam. If you look over the wall at the beginning you will see up close the plughole-design drain which lets the water flow from the reservoir. **2** Once you have crossed the dam, pass through the gate and turn right onto the tarmac path.

Keep your dogs on the leads until you reach the end of the dam wall, as they may jump over thinking that it is level on the other side. Follow this wooded path along the edge of the water. There may be sheep grazing so keep your dog under close control.

The path will ascend and descend, moving away from the water's edge at times. You will pass the odd bay for forestry vehicles to turn around. Ignore several paths to your left. Continue for some distance. You will reach a stone wall on your right, and shortly afterwards you will pass two disused stone gate posts on your left.

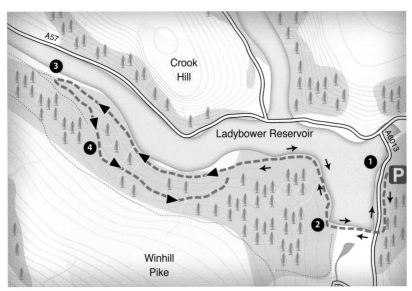

You will pass well-spaced beech trees on your left. You will come to a larger vehicle-turning area, passing three tracks on your right entering into it, The area is close to the water, with grassy areas. After passing this you will climb higher above the water.

The path will descend again, where you will see the reservoir once more. Just after the path begins another ascent, look out for a path left and back, ascending diagonally into the forest. It is indicated by a yellow way marker. ❸ This path will become a little steeper and there are remnants of an old stone wall on the right. It is mostly covered in moss and grasses.

You will reach a track where you go straight ahead to continue ascending into the forest. You will see the yellow way marker to help you find your way. ❹ Once reaching another track don't go through the gate but go left beside the enclosed plantation, following the grassy track.

You will have lovely views left of the hills as you look over the forest clearing and the stock fence to your right. Once you leave the stock fence you will return into the forest.

The path will soon descend again as it cuts through the hillside. Just before the path levels out, there is a sharp left bend where a track descends. Ignore this track and continue straight ahead. Continue on this track for some distance. On reaching another path, turn right onto a familiar path and continue the way that you came back to your car.

14. Wyming Brook

Medium - 4.2 miles - 2hrs

This is a fantastic circular walk descending through a truly stunning valley, which has beautiful woodland with ferns covering the ground, many rocky boulders and rock faces. You will follow Wyming Brook, which has many waterfalls and bridges to cross as the river meanders along the valley floor. Further on an ascent brings amazing views across the moorland to the hills beyond. The path can get a little rough in places. There may be sheep grazing in parts but there are no roads and plenty of water along the way.

How to get there – After passing the Ladybower Reservoir stay on the A57 heading towards Sheffield, ignoring a left turn signed for the M1 (North). Take the next right hand turn onto Lodge Lane. At the junction turn right onto Redmires Road. Continue along this road for some distance where you will pass a 'No Through Road' sign. You will see the car park on your right a little further along the road.

Grid Reference – SK 269858

Parking – Free in the car park

Facilities – There are no facilities

You will need – Dog lead, dog bags

The Walk

❶ From the car park, go to the furthest end from the road and take the path straight ahead and to the right, descending to the brook. Cross the stepping stones over the brook. Ascend a couple of steps then take the path on the left.

Follow alongside the brook through the woodland with rocky outcrops on your right. Follow the brook descending into the valley, crossing many bridges as the river meanders between the boulders.

After some time the path will become higher than the river below and it will veer to the left. There is a bench at a clearing in the woods. You will then descend steps, just before reaching a kissing gate. Pass through the kissing gate and turn left. **❷**

Ascend on the old disused road, which is also a bridleway. Ignore a path on the left and continue on the wooded path. On meeting another path, turn right, passing a sandstone retainer wall, following signs for Reddicar Clough. You can alternatively take the path on the left, which will bring you back to the car park.

Continue through the mixed woodland, ignoring a path on the left. Again a

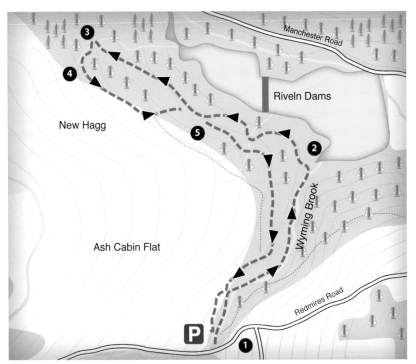

little further along, ignore another path on the left and continue following signs for A57. You will pass a low stone wall on the right. Be aware that there is a drop on the other side. Ensure your dog doesn't jump over by keeping him under close control or on a lead.

You will pass a rock outcrop on the left and then a section of silver birch woods with thick bilberry covering the woodland floor to your left. There is another low stone wall on your right, so keep your dog close. There are a few sections of wall ahead, but not all have a drop on the other side.

Ignore another path on the left as you reach a bridge. ❸ Cross the bridge and then turn left, into woods with the river on your left. Dogs can cool off here, providing that the river isn't too fast flowing. Check this before allowing him access.

The woodland is stunning here, dominated by oak and silver birch to begin with and then mixed deciduous trees. There are rocky outcrops as you pass. Some way along you will cross a footbridge and then ascend between bilberries on the worn path over exposed bedrock. There may be sheep grazing in the area, so ensure that you have your dog under close control or on a lead. Pass through a kissing gate.

Cross an expanse of heathland, keeping your dog on the path during the nesting season. On reaching a way marker, turn left. ❹ Continue across the heath, which is truly stunning when the heather is in flower in August/ September.

Pass through a kissing gate and turn immediately right. You will reach another kissing gate. Don't go through this, but turn left, following the worn path descending through bracken. The bracken can enclose the path in places. You will pass through woodland once again, with bracken and bilberry understory. You will reach a familiar path: turn right here, signed Rivelin Dams. Ignore a path on the right and continue. You will see a familiar path on the left on reaching the stone embankment. Ignore this and follow on the path, which is also a bridleway signed to the car park. ❺

The path cuts through the hillside amongst woodland. Ignore the path right, which goes up a ladder, and continue on a gentle ascent to begin with, which then becomes steeper. You will hear the sound of the brook below on your left. The wall on your left has quite a drop on the other side in places, so keep your dog under close control. Pass lots of exposed rock on your right, and when the stone wall ends you will see the brook down below. The path will soon return to the car park.

15. Stanage Edge

Easy - 4 miles - 2hrs

This is a super linear walk alongside the famous cliff face known as Stanage Edge. The rock formations are fantastic and very typical of the Dark Peak. There are stunning views across this wonderful landscape. There may be sheep throughout this walk and during March through to the end of July there may be ground-nesting birds. This walk is particularly fantastic during August when the heather is in flower, and cotton grass blankets the ground in early summer. There are no roads except for the beginning and end.

How to get there - From Hathersage, head towards Sheffield on the A6187. Just outside Hathersage, turn left when you see signs for Ringinglow. Follow this road, passing a road on your left and continue until you reach the car park on your right.

Grid Reference – SK 259829

Parking – Free in Burbage Bridge car park

Facilities – There are no facilities

You will need – Dog leads, dog bags

The Walk

❶ From the car park, go back onto the road, cross over and turn left. Continue along the path at the side of the road. On reaching a left bend in the road, continue straight ahead along the well-worn path, passing a sandstone block. A little further along there is a water-hole on the right of the path. This is small but quite deep. In hot weather if your dog goes in you may have to help him out.

Please keep your dog on a lead during nesting season and lambing times. Nesting season is from the beginning of March until the end of July. Dogs can easily scare off birds or kill young chicks that nest on the ground. The open landscape is stunning in early- to mid-summer as there are masses of white cotton grass. In August and September the heather is a mass of purple.

Head towards the large rock outcrops, known as Stanage Edge. When you reach close to the outcrops, follow the path, stepping up and over the exposed rock. **❷** You will reach stone flags a little further along. Then cross over more rocks, where you will pass a trig-point on your left. It is worth climbing to the trig-point for stunning views across the landscape and looking along the edge of the rock outcrop.

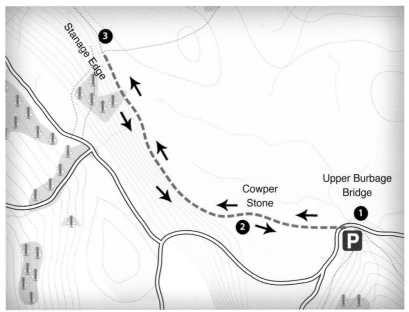

Some of the outcrops are high and therefore there is a drop on the other side. Continue along the rock or on the path to your right. After a while, you will reach a dilapidated stone wall on your right. Follow beside the wall and a little further along, pass through a gap in the stone wall.

Continue along the top ridge, passing a path on your left that descends between rocks. Continue beside the stone wall on your right. At the end of the stone wall, ignore a couple of paths on the right. The path becomes less rocky now; continue on until you reach a metal post, where the path begins to descend.

❸ This is your turning point. You will have new views as you head back in the opposite direction.

Retrace your steps, staying on the top path. On returning to the trig-point you will see your path back down to the car park. Keep the post and rail fences on your left as you descend the rocky sections. Remember to put your dog on a lead, before reaching the road.

16. Hathersage

Medium - 5.2 miles - 2hrs 30min

A wonderful circular walk, following the River Derwent, passing through meadows and then beside farm fields, with lovely mature trees growing along the river bank. The walk then passes through beautiful countryside, along quiet lanes climbing to reach fantastic views of the rolling hills and the fabulous rocky ridge of Stanage Edge. You will then pass through lovely woodland. There are quiet roads and livestock along this walk. Your dog will find lots of water along the way.

How to get there – On reaching the village of Hathersage from the main road, turn onto Station Road and then turn left onto Oddfellows Road, where the car park will be on your left.

Grid Reference – SK 231813 Nearest **Postcode** – S32 1DU

Parking – Pay and display

Facilities – There is a café and tea room opposite the car park

You will need – Dog lead and dog bags

The Walk

1 From the car park turn right on the road and then left. Turn right onto Dove Lane. After passing the houses, pass under a railway bridge. You will reach a stone house, Nether Hall, built in 1873. Turn left, just before the house, keeping your dog on the lead, as there are free range hens.

Stay on the wide path to the edge of the field, with a hedgerow on your right. At the end of the field, pass through a gate and continue along the path. There are super mature oak and ash trees. The hedgerow will end and you will just have a stock fence between the fields.

Before reaching the end of the field, ensure you have your dog on a lead, pass through a gate and then a gap in the stone wall to reach a road. Turn right and cross a road bridge over the river Derwent. **2** Go through a gap in the stone wall and then through a gate onto a footpath signed Shatton. You may need to keep your dog on a lead or under close control as there may be livestock grazing.

Continue along the worn path, beside the river on your right. There are mature alder trees lining the edge of the river and there is a meadow on your left. Pass through a gate, entering Goose Nest Wood. Continue along the path beside the river, with a wooded slope and mixed deciduous trees on your left.

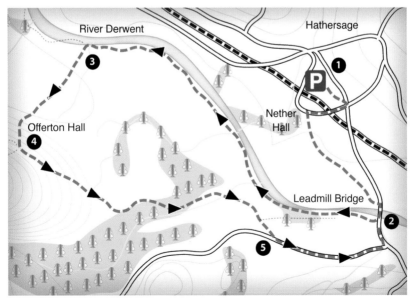

After a little while, you will leave the woodland, crossing a footbridge over a stream. There is farmland now to your left, with a stock fence. Pass through a gate and then cross another footbridge over a stream. There are lovely views ahead of the hilly countryside and wild flowers line the path in the summer months.

You will see Nether Hall on the opposite side of the river, just as the path bends to the left. There are many gates to pass through with stock fences on the left. If you have your dog off the lead, be sure that as you go through the gates there is adequate, secure stock fencing on the other side. There may also be sheep on the path. Check that the stock fence is secure, and if it is not or if there is an open gate into the stock field keep your dog on a lead or under close control.

❸ On reaching a way marker take the left turn, signed Offerton. Pass through the gate into farmland, where livestock may be grazing so keep your dog under close control, and cross the field, close to the line of mature trees in the hedgerow on your right, ascending on the worn grassy path.

On reaching a gate in the stone wall, turn around and look at the stunning views across the beautiful landscape. Pass through the gate and proceed through the middle of a field, ascending the worn path in the gully.

On reaching another gate, turn around and rest for a while, as you take in the splendid scene. Stanage Edge can be seen just below the skyline. Trees line the fields giving that patchwork effect across the countryside. To your right, you can seeBurbage Rockss.

Pass through the gate and continue straight ahead, along the grassy track, between the stock fences. Go through another gate, continue straight ahead and then turn left onto a quiet lane, passing Offerton Hall. ❹ Follow the bend left as the road ascends. You will pass two footpaths on the right and then

continue, with sloping fields and a stock fence on your right and a stone wall on your left.

The road begins to descend. Just before the sharp bend to the right and the woodland, take the footpath on the left, passing through the gate to avoid the cattle grid to reach Callow House.

Ignore a footpath on your left and pass the house on your left. Take the small gate straight ahead, and descend, passing through a gap in the stone wall. Ensure your dog is under close control as there are livestock grazing, then descend the steps and then a hill to reach a gate. Pass through the gate into woods.

Follow the obvious path through mixed coniferous and deciduous woodland. At the end of the woods pass through a kissing gate, where livestock may be grazing. Follow the path, which cuts across slopes in the field, heading for a gate on the opposite side.

Pass through the gate and turn right ascending on the farm track. Put your dog on a lead, as there is a road ahead. ❺ On reaching the quiet road, turn left, ignoring a footpath on your left. You will descend and then ascend once more.

You will reach another quiet road. Turn left here and descend until you reach Leadmill Village. There is a busy road here, so ensure your dog is on a lead. On reaching the road, turn left and cross a familiar road bridge.

Turn left onto the footpath once again, following the field edge, with the stock fence on your left. Remember, even if there are no livestock in the field, there are free range hens. Turn right on reaching Nether Hall and at the end of the road turn left. Take the next right into Oddfellows Road to return to the car park.

17. Higger Tor

Medium - 2.5 miles - 2hrs

A wonderful circular walk, passing some fabulous exposed rock faces with amazing shapes, carved over the millennia by the sweeping winds. You will pass wonderful heathland and follow alongside a forest as you travel along Burbage Brook, where your dog can cool off. There are some rock boulders to climb down, but they are no more difficult than large steps. There are cliff edges and sheep may be grazing throughout the walk. There may also be ground-nesting birds during March to the end of July. The walk is for agile people only and you may need to head towards land marks when the paths are a little un-clear. After periods of rain, it may be tricky to cross the river.

How to get there - From Hathersage, head towards Sheffield on the A6187. Just outside Hathersage turn left when you see signs for Ringinglow. Follow this road, until you reach the lay-by on your left.

Grid Reference – SK 256822

Parking – Free in the lay-by

Facilities – There are no facilities

You will need – Dog lead and a clear day

The Walk

❶ From the lay-by cross to the opposite side of the road, pass through the gate and follow the well-worn footpath. Keep to the main path, passing amongst the rocky boulders. There are cliff edges as you ascend to meet the rock faces, so keep your dog under close control.

You can seeBurbage Rocks face on your left in the distance. The path ascends over flat exposed rock. There are pockets of ling between the rocks, and heather, cotton grass and ling blanket the slope on your right. You will walk amongst stunning rock formations, which the wind has created over many years, reflecting a typical landscape of the Dark Peak.

❷ Keep going straight ahead over the rocky outcrop, where you will lose the path for a short while, as you choose your path across the rock. There are several ways down, but if you veer to the right, you may find it a little easier. You will see the path ahead of you once again as you climb down the rock. You will reach steps to descend to the path.

On reaching the path again, continue straight ahead, through the moorland. Ignore a worn, grassy path on your left, and a few paces on, just as the path starts to ascend towards another rock face, take the grassy path on the left. You will see another rock outcrop on your far right.

As you descend, you will be enclosed by the bracken. There are several paths here, which end up at the same wider path ahead. The one on the left is a little wider and may be the best one to choose. You are heading for the end of the furthest tree plantation ahead of you.

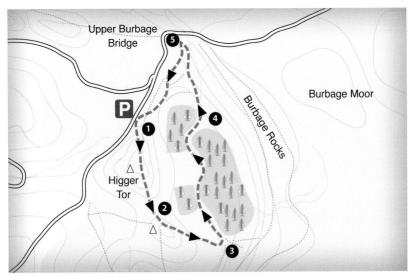

You will pass over a stream, then the path widens out. Continue heading for the end of the plantation at the bottom of the valley, between the bracken and glacial boulders. You will reach a fantastic arched bridge, with stone slabs on the top, crossing over a river.

❸ Cross the bridge and turn left following the narrow path, between the river and the tree plantation. Your dog can get access to the river here to cool off. The trees are low in places, so watch your head. Follow beside the plantation for some distance, on a gentle ascent, crossing a rocky section and a stream, listening only to the birds and running water.

Just before reaching the end of the plantation, after descending into a dip, take a path on your left which gradually descends to the river, crossing the boulders to the other side (if the river is too high you may find another spot further along the river). Turn right and continue, following the river on your right and another plantation on your left. **❹** A little further along, the path veers away from the river and ascends a little more steeply, with exposed rock in places. Bracken will dominate the area ahead. Ignore a path on your left, keeping to the right. You will meet with a wet/boggy area, but you can cross over the bedrock to avoid this.

The path will cross more exposed bedrock for some distance. As the path changes to gravel, you will see a fence line ahead with a car park beyond. Just before reaching the fence and a kissing gate, turn left to join a path which switches back in the opposite direction for a while, ascending to reach exposed bedrock.

Ignore a grassy path which veers to the left, and continue with the exposed bedrock, where you will reach more cliff edges. Descend the rocky boulders for a short section and then the path levels out. Follow a grassy path, heading back towards Higger Tor, on a path which cuts across the hillside.

The path ascends again, and on reaching a post turn right on a narrow path cutting across the moor. On reaching another path turn right, descending back towards the road and the lay-by where you have parked your car.

18. Burbage Rocks

Medium - 4.2 miles - 2hrs

This is a brilliant circular walk, passing amongst some amazing rock crags. There are wonderful panoramic views, after only a short ascent. You will be amongst heather, bilberry, white cotton grass and bracken and once at the top ofBurbage Rocks you will have moorland as far as the eye can see. There are cliff faces and sheep throughout, with ground-nesting birds between 1st March – 31st July. There are some rocky areas to pass over, but no scrambling is required.

How to get there – From Hathersage, head towards Sheffield on the A6187. Just outside Hathersage turn left when you see signs for Ringinglow. Follow this road, passing a road on your left and continue until you reach the car park on your right.

Grid Reference – SK 259829

Parking – Free in Burbage Bridge car park

Facilities – There are no facilities

You will need – Dog leads

The Walk

1 From the car park, face the stock fencing, with the entrance on your left. Take the kissing gate on your right at the end of the first parking bay. Keep your dog on a lead or under close control as there are sheep grazing. On passing through the gate, turn left and head towards the road bridge.

Descend on the worn path and then pass over some rocky areas, crossing Burbage Brook, which flows through the tunnel. Your dog can take a cooling drink here. The path then ascends as you walk above the stone rock face, close to the stock fence. Pass another tunnel, as you cross another river, and continue to ascend, passing a kissing gate on your left. The path will then gently descend, passing rock faces known asBurbage Rocks. The area is dominated by bracken, with pockets of cotton grass and heather. Several streams pass under the path, where your dog can get a drink.

The views in all directions are fabulous, with the wooded valley, hills and stunning, sculptured boulders and rock crags, which are very popular for climbing and bouldering. The path will level out, where you continue for some distance. You will pass a way marker on your left and then a little further along a path on your right. The path will get a little rough and it will descend gradually once again. You will pass between old, stone gate posts, and you will see a road on your right. Put your dog on a lead and continue on the path, where you will reach a kissing gate. Pass through the kissing gate,

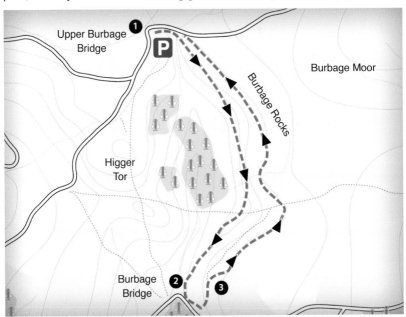

and then pass beside a gate, into a small car park. ❷ As you reach near to the road, take a footpath on your left, turning left again almost immediately. Pass through a gate and then under a mature oak tree. Ascend the path with heather, ling, bilberry and bracken. The path will soon level out, and down below on your left you can see the path on which you have already trodden.

Passing rock boulders that are strewn across the landscape, you will reach a fork in the path. Take the right path and ascend a little more. Pass a stone block, with a channel carved out on the top. Sit here and take a rest on the long stone. ❸ The views are fantastic, with rocks stacked on top of one another on the horizon. Continue on your ascent and as you climb you will cross over flat boulders that resemble giant pebbles. Keep your dog under close control as you will pass rock faces on your left, with big drops on the other side.

On reaching the rock faces, you will have reached moorland on your right, with large expanses of cotton grass and heather. The path follows the tops of the rock faces on your left. Remember there may be ground-nesting birds on the moorland, depending on the time of year. After passing the first rock face, the path descends a little. Look out for a path on your left, which passes between cairns (rock piles, used to define the path). Follow this path, passing amongst the heather. The path veers to the right and you will then pass over a stream.

The path will ascend gradually, amongst bracken and passing over exposed bedrock. Pick your way around the rocky sections, heading for the exposed rock face ahead. Continue to follow on the worn path, where you will eventually reach the second rock face, bringing you stunning views of the distinctive landscape of the Peak District.

Follow the grassy path and on leaving the rock faces the landscape opens out, with vast moorland on your right and in the distance. The cotton grasses, when in flower look like white blankets across the landscape. You will soon see the car park ahead. The path descends and passes a car park on your right, then crosses the stream, where your dog can get another drink and cool off in the water. Continue on the familiar path, back to the car park ahead.

Countryside Dog Walks - Peak District, North (Dark Peak Area)

19. Surprise View

Medium - 1.2 miles - 45mins

This is a super circular walk, with the most amazing views. You will walk amongst the heather on well-made paths, where after a gradual, easy ascent you will reach some amazing rock faces with interesting shapes, sculpted by the wind. August is the best time to see heather in bloom, where it stretches out its purple blanket across the landscape. There are sheep grazing, so you will need to keep your dog under close control or on a lead. During the nesting season there may also be ground-nesting birds. There are no roads.

How to get there – Take the A6187 from Hathersage towards Sheffield. Shortly after leaving the village Surprise View car park will be located on the left hand side of the road.

Grid Reference – SK 251801

Parking – Pay and Display

Facilities – There are no facilities

You will need – Dog leads, dog bags, and water for your dog in hot weather

The Walk

❶ On entering the car park, turn left until you reach the end of the car park and go through the gate, keeping your dog on a lead or under close control as there may be sheep grazing and ground-nesting birds. Follow the stone path between the heather.

There are silver birch trees on your right and scattered, rocky boulders. On reaching another gate, pass through it and follow the path, where you will reach a view point. On a clear day you will have fabulous panoramic views. **❷**

Return back through the gate and turn left, following the worn path beside the stock fence. Ignore a gate on your left and continue on a gradual ascent, passing over exposed bedrock in places. Pass another gate on your left, and as you climb higher you will pass some cliff edges on your left. The views over the stock fence are completely stunning.

After passing over an exposed rocky section the views are expanded in every direction. You leave the worn path, where ahead you will have views of Stanage Edge on the left and Higger Tor on your right. Now take the grassy path on your right, heading towards the rock face.

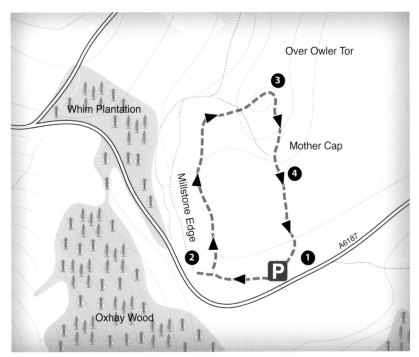

You will pass large rocks as you go, some with puddles if there has been recent rainfall, where your dog can get a drink. As you near the rock face bracken dominates. On reaching the rock face veer to your left a little and cross over the top, stepping over the rock.

❸ On reaching the top, you will find a path for your return if you go towards the mushroom-shaped rock. First of all you can have a rest and explore the rock faces. Once on the path next to the mushroom-shaped rock, descend on the well-defined path, heading for the rock stack.

❹ Go around the stack, where you will pick up the path once again. Continue on the path between the heather, passing some interesting rock shapes, with a millstone or two amongst them. Descend over some exposed rock, and look for a path on your right after passing between the silver birch trees.

Take the path on your right, descending a little more steeply over some exposed rock, into the silver birch woodland with bracken understory. Sheep may still be present in the woodland. You will soon see the car park straight ahead. Put your dog on a lead before entering the car park.

20. Blacka Woods   Medium - 2.7 miles - 1hr 30min

This is a lovely walk, mostly in beautiful mixed woodland, where the majority of the walk is free from grazing sheep. There are some open areas that may be grazed occasionally. There are streams passing through in several places where your dog can have a cooling drink. If you do this walk in August – September the heathland section of the walk is a wonderful mass of purple. There are a few ascents and you may encounter horses and cyclists in sections of the walk, whilst walking along the bridleways. If you go during nesting season, keep your dog on the path to avoid disturbance to ground-nesting birds as you cross a short section of moor.

How to get there –Take the A6187 out of Hathersage, heading towards Sheffield. You will pass the Fox House pub on your left and then after passing a road on your right, you will see the car park on your right at the side of the road, immediately before a block of trees.

Grid Reference – SK 277805
Nearest Postcode – S17 3AH

Parking – Free in the car park

Facilities – There are no facilities

You will need – Dog leads, dog bags

Countryside Dog Walks - Peak District, North (Dark Peak Area)

The Walk

❶ Keep dogs on the lead to begin with as the path runs parallel with the road and the wall is dilapidated in places. From the car park go through the gate way in the stone wall, entering into the mixed deciduous woodland with some Scots pine. Follow the worn path, ignoring a path on your right a little further along.

Keep your dog under close control and pass through a gate on reaching a stone wall. Continue on the path, with a stone wall on your left. A little further on, pass an exit onto the road on your left and continue straight ahead, ignoring a path on your right. The path will soon veer away from the road. The trees become more widely spaced for a short section, with bilberry and bracken understory.

Ignore a path on the right and then the path will descend gradually and get a little rough with some eroded gullies and stone. There are some wonderful mature trees throughout the woodland. **❷** On reaching another path, turn right, continuing with a gradual descent. As you descend more steeply, the path gets a little rockier.

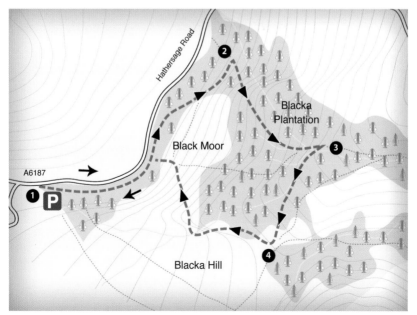

As you reach level ground pass over a small ravine in the woodland, with ferns dominating the woodland floor. Continue on a descent, passing a stream on the right, where dogs can get a drink and cool off. Silver birch, rowan and alder trees dominate this section of woodland.

Cross a footbridge over a stream and turn left, on level ground for a short spell, then descending once again. Pass through an old gateway with stone gate posts. **❸** Take the path on your right, where there is a stream for dogs to cool off. Cross the stream, via the stones. Continue along the well made path, ascending for quite a distance.

Just before reaching a wider track and two benches on your right, turn right on a narrow path. **❹** Ascend gradually, walking between the bracken. You will have views to your right, over the surrounding countryside and hills.

You will pass some exposed rock, with a river below on your right and after rainfall you will see a small waterfall. Ignore a path on your left and continue, where you will reach a stream crossing. Pass through a small section of trees and after passing a Ramblers Association plaque you will reach a section of moorland.

Cross this, keeping dogs on the path during nesting season. In the late summer months this is a fantastic sight, covered in purple heather, with bilberry, and purple moor grass. There are extensive views on your right. On reaching another path, close to the edge of woodland, turn left. Ascend the path, keeping your dog under close control or on a lead, as there is a road ahead.

You will reach a gate. Don't go through it, but turn left, where you are now on a familiar path. This path will lead back to the car park. Remember to keep dogs under close control for the last section as the wall has gaps onto a busy road. There isn't a gate on reaching the car park, next to the busy road, so dogs will need to be on a lead well before you return.

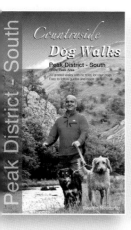

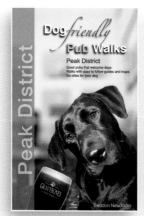

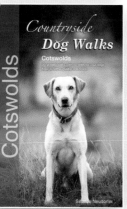

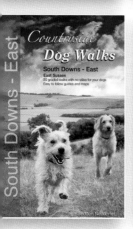

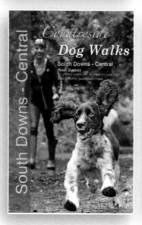

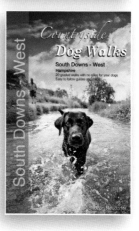

www.countrysidedogwalks.co.uk

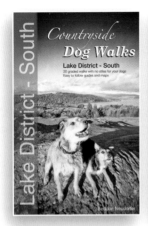
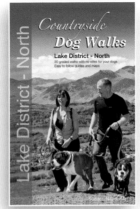
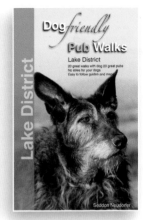
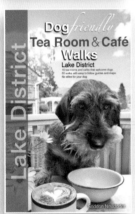
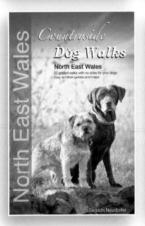

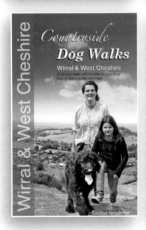
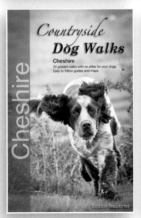
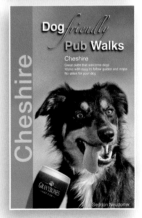